Finding N :
The Great
Alphabet Hunt

Paula Curtis Taylorson

illustrated by **Marharyta Serebrianska**

Finding N : The Great Alphabet Hunt

This is a work of fiction.

Text and Illustrations copyrighted

by Paula Curtis Taylorson ©2022

Library of Congress Control Number: 2021905038

All rights reserved. No part of this book may be

reproduced, transmitted, or stored in an information retrieval

system in any form or by any means,

graphic, electronic, or mechanical without prior written

permission from the author.

Printed in the United States of America

A 2 Z Press LLC

PO Box 582

Deleon Springs, FL 32130

bestlittleonlinebookstore.com

sizemore3630@aol.com

440-241-3126

ISBN: 978-1-954191-15-0

Dedication

Thank you to those who read to me and those who listened to me read.

This book belongs to:

_____

It's late one **noiseless November** evening.
Nicholas the **night** watchman
is starting on his round.

He's searching out words
that begin with **N**,

and keeping the **neighbourhood** safe and sound!

He looks **neat** in his **navy** blue uniform, with his **nifty necktie**.

He **noses** through gardens
and **nips** into parks and the roads,
flashing his torch into
all the **nooks** and crannies,

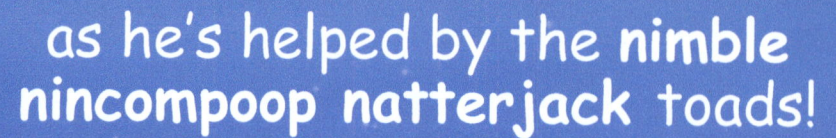

as he's helped by the **nimble nincompoop natterjack** toads!

Those **notorious natterjack** toads wear **newspaper night** caps

and **nod** as they follow
in a **northerly** line,
nudging and bumping
against each other

The **Nocturnal** animals
are all **now** awake.

And the **nefarious** badger
triplets **Neville**, **Nigel**, and **Nancy**

nosh on nettles, nectarines, and nuts,

as an owl hoots from his **nest** in the **needle** pine tree.

A **nightingale** from **Nashville**
sings country and western.
She is **nonchalant** and
a **natural** at rhythm and blues.

Nicholas notices
some **newts** doing a
new-fangled line dance,

and a **nightcrawler named Norman** is **nicely** polishing his shoes,

A **narwhal** called **Nellie** lives
on a **nautical** **narrowboat**.
She reads a **novel** and **naps** in a
hammock made of from old **nets**.

She wears a **Navajo necklace** of musical **notes** around her **neck**

A **neon** sign let's us know the **nearby** café is soon closing,

so **Nicholas negotiates** his food purchase with the owner whose **nickname** is Ned.

Nicholas enjoys his nutritious parcel of midnight nibbles of noodles and nachos and delicious naan bread !

On **Nineth** Street, the **natterjack** toads hear **numerous** sounds. It's **normal** and **natural** for **new-born** babies to cry.

In the **night** sky,
Neptune is shining.
Nicholas says we **navigate**
by the **North** star. .

And below, Lord **Nelson** stands high on his column, looking down at the **news** readers driving **new** cars.

There's an old **nag** who is dressed like a **ninja**. She does **needlework** and eats **nutmeg** by the light of the moon,

While she waits for her
niece and her **nephew**,
and **Nugget** their **naughty** pet
numbat, who's a bit like a raccoon.

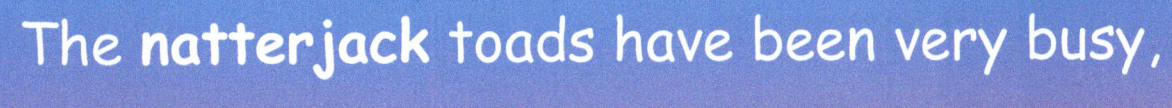

The **natterjack** toads have been very busy,

Seeking **Ns** in the dark of the **night**.

They Keep looking on until the **next** morning,

When the fifteenth letter is in sight! (O)

The End

My Very Own 'N' Words:

_____

_____

_____

_____

_____

_____

_____

_____

_____

_____

_____

Glossary

Page 1. **Noiseless** : silent, quiet
November : a month of the year
Nicholas : a boy or man's name
Night watchman - a person who guards
or protects from fire, theft, crime

Page 2. **N** : a letter

Page 3. **Neighborhood** : an area where people live
Also on page 3. **Nanny goat** : a farm animal

Page 4. **Neat** : orderly, clean, clever,
pleasant
Navy : dark blue color
Nifty : very good, fine, stylish, fun
Necktie : small strip of clothing
worn around the neck

Page 5. **Noses/nosing** : investigates, search,
Nips/nipping : to sneak into
or roam around in
Nooks : small spaces

Page 6. **Nimble** : flexible, talented
Nincompoop : silly acting, clownish
Natterjack toads : is a toad that lives in the sandy areas of Europe
The adults have a yellow line down the middle of the back
The toads are an endangered species and are
 protected under the 1981 Wildlife and Countryside Act
They have short hind legs and run rather than hop

Page 7. **Notorious** : well-known, famous
Newspaper : special paper with stories
of local events and weather
Nightcaps : a head covering while sleeping

Page 8. **Nod** : a quick or slight
lowering of the head
Northerly : direction to the North
Nudging : push or touch slightly or gently

Page 9. **Noisily** : with much sound
Nine : a number

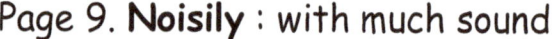

Page 10. **Nocturnal** - occurring at night time
Now : the present time or moment, immediate

Page 11. **Nefarious** : villainous, mischievous
Neville : a boy or man's name
Nigel : a boy or man's name
Nancy : a girl or woman's name

Page 12. **Nosh** : snack or eat
between meals
Nectarine : fruit
Nectarines : fruit
Nuts : food

Page 13. **Nest** : a pocket-like area for laying eggs of birds or reptiles
Needle pine tree : stiff, slender projections on a pine tree

Page 14. **Nightingale** - a bird
Nashville : a city in Tennessee, USA
Nonchalant : casual, no hurry
Natural : common, expected

Page 15. **Notices** : to become aware of
Newts : little salamanders
New - fangled : something newly discovered, done newfangled

Page 16. **Nightcrawlers** : worms
Named : a word to identify someone
Norman : a boy or man's name
Nicely : to be kind and gentle

Page 17. **Narwhal** : a whale
Nellie : a girl or woman's name
Nautical : pertaining to the sea or water
Narrowboat : not wide, the sides are close together for this sea craft
Novel : a book
Naps : short sleep
Nets : lace-like or mesh-like bags to catch things in

Page 18. **Navajo necklace** : jewelry made on a chain or rope to wear around the neck made by Navajo Indians
Notes : small round black spots to designate musical sound
Neck : the area of the body under the head

Page 19. . **Newfoundland** : a country, a dog
Name ; what someone is called

Page 20. **Neon** : brightly shining light
Nearby : close

Page 21. **Negotiates** : to agree on a price
Nickname : a fun name given to someone in place of their proper name
Ned : a boy or man's name

Page 22. **Nutritious** : good and healthy food
Nibbles : small bites, snacks
Noodles : food, pasta
Nachos : food, crackers
Naan bread : flat bread

Page 23. **Ninth** : referring to number nine
Numerous : many
Normal : usual, expected, common,
Natural : normal, usual
New-born : young, recently born

Page 24. **Nanny** : one hired to care for children
Nylon : a type of fabric for clothing
Night gown : dress or shirt worn for sleeping
Nurse : one hired to care for children or sick people
Nightmare : bad or frightening dream

Page 25. **Night sky** :
Neptune : a planet in the sky
Navigate : finding one's way, direction

Page 26. **Lord Nelson** :
News : written reports, information, intelligent
New : original, recent

Page 27. **Nearby** : close to
Nag : an happy older woman
Ninja : pertaining to Japanese martial arts
Needlework : to sew creatively
Nutmeg : a spice

Page 28. **Niece** : the daughter of a brother or sister
Nephew : the son of a brother or sister
Nugget : a name given to a pet (here)
Naughty : misbehaving
Numbat : small animal like a raccoon

Page 31. **Next** : to follow the present thing or person

Paula Curtis-Taylorson Lives in Marston Mortaine England. She is a full-time secondary school teacher of English and English Literature. She was amongst the first of the initial students to graduate from the Uk's first BA (Hons) Creative Writing Program at the University of Bedfordshire.

Her first love is poetry and rhyme and she works hard to inspire and teach appreciation of the subject to all age groups. Many of her students have gone on to be successful writers.

A2Z Press LLC

A2Z Press LLC
published this work.
A2Z Press LLC is a
publishing company
created by Terrie Sizemore
for the purpose
of publishing literary works by new
and aspiring writers. All content is
G-rated. We welcome your submissions
of ideas for children's literature as well
as adult and self-help topics.
Science and medicine, holidays and
other interesting topics are all welcome.
Submit queries to sizemore3630@aol.com or
PO Box 582
Deleon Springs, FL 32130

www.ingramcontent.com/pod-product-compliance
Lightning Source LLC
Chambersburg PA
CBHW041523120626
46551CB00018B/2546